MY FIRST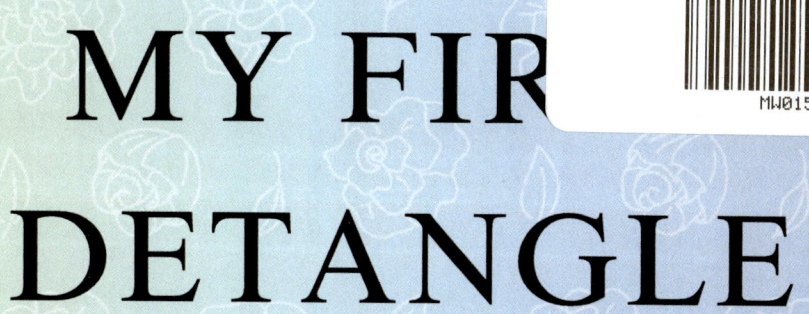
DETANGLE

Written by Aisha Motley.

Illustrated by Prolific Palms Design Co.

MY FIRST DETANGLE!

By Aisha Motley
Illustrated by Prolific Palms Design CO.
Published 2025

Copyright 2025 Aisha Motley.

All rights reserved. This book or any portion thereof may not be reproduced or used in any manner whatsoever without the express written permission of the publisher except for the use of brief quotations in a book review.

Printed by Illustrations by Prolific Palms Design Co in the United States of America

About the Author

Aisha is a hairstylist located in Sacramento, California. She has two cats and is born and raised in Sacramento. She's had a love for curls since a child. Growing up with two older sisters, hair was something that brought the family together and still does for many. Straight out of high school, She started cosmetology school and fell in love with the idea of changing someone's confidence just by a hairstyle. Working with men and women, teaching the simple steps of creating easy, workable curls is her passion. She hopes to have more books in the future and is excited to educate more people on the techniques to make curly hair not a bother.

Made in the USA
Coppell, TX
01 February 2026

My First Detangle, is a tutorial explaining how to take care of curly and coily hair. The process of shampooing, conditioning, sectioning, and detangling is all explained throughout the book. This is a great beginners book for friends looking to learn more about the art of coily hair. Tools products and quick tips, help you to make detangling a breeze. Taking care of your natural hair has never been easier!

ACKNOWLEDGEMENTS

Creating this book has been a wonderful journey, and it wouldn't have been possible without the support and encouragement of many wonderful people.

I would like to express my deepest gratitude to the amazing individuals with beautiful curly hair who inspired this book. Your unique curls and vibrant personalities are the heart and soul of these pages.

To my family and friends, thank you for your unwavering support and belief in this project. Your love and encouragement have kept me going every step of the way.

I am also deeply grateful to the talented illustrator whose wonderful artwork captures the magic and beauty of curly hair. Your creativity and attention to detail have made this book a visual delight.

Finally, to all the young readers and their families, thank you for welcoming this book into your homes and hearts. May it inspire you to embrace and celebrate your unique curls and the beauty that comes with them.

With heartfelt gratitude,
Aisha Motley.

Table of Contents

 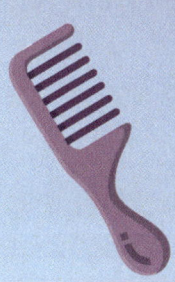

Introduction 1

What you need 5

Wash Day 7

Sectioning 10

Detangling 13

Activity Pages 17

You have been blessed with gorgeous curls and coils! Such a gift deserves proper care and attention. Let's enjoy ourselves and discover how to maintain them beautifully!

These are your guides Matthew, Lisa, and Monique! They will give you Quick Tips and let you know what's needed for each page!

Matthew **Lisa** **Monique**

Hair is a beautiful thing, but sometimes things don't go as planned, the results of this tutorial may vary based on your individual hair. We encourage you to experiment and adjust the methods to suit your specific hair needs for the best results. Always consider your hair's health and consult with a professional if you're unsure about the techniques or products that are right for you.

Always remember practice makes perfect!

We hear a lot about hair pattern but your hair pattern, is not the only way to define how healthy your hair is or how it will act. It also doesn't truly tell you how to take care of it. If looking for the best way to work with you hair you'll look at the texture, porosity, and hair density!

What is hair pattern?

Hair patterns include straight, wavy, curly, and coily, they can influence how hair looks. If your hair has a spiral curl, loose wave, or tight coil, that is the pattern of your hair.

What is hair texture?

Hair texture describes the thickness of a person's hair strands and can range from fine to medium to coarse.

What is hair density?

Hair density is the amount of hair strands on the scalp . It refers to how closely packed the hairs are, ranging from low density (thin) , medium density, high density (thick).

What is hair porosity?

Hair porosity is the hair's ability to absorb and retain moisture. This can be affected by heat styling, colored treated or bleached hair, and the environment. Hair can be low porosity (resistant to moisture), medium porosity (balanced moisture retention), or high porosity (allowing quick moisture absorption but also quick loss).

Pro Tip:
Once you're used to the technique you can add a rat tail comb and try butterfly clips for sectioning.

Let's begin by identifying what tools we will need to start with! A bristle brush that is soft on the hair is very important. When shopping for a brush make sure it says it is for curly hair and you will see a big difference.

Having a wide tooth comb is essential to your hair routine. It can be used for sectioning and for detangling.

Hair ties are needed for sectioning and can be used to create styles by securing the hair in place.

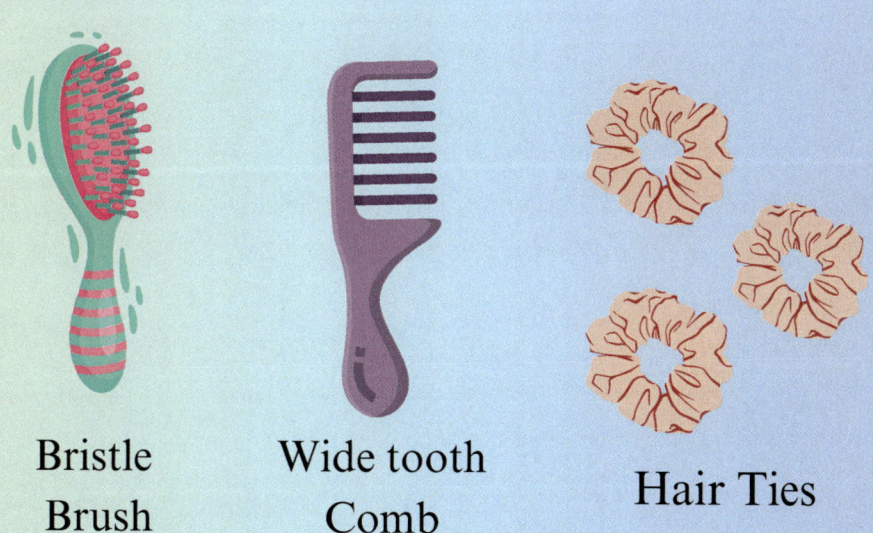

Bristle Brush   Wide tooth Comb   Hair Ties

There is a wide variety of products available, but only four are essential for maintaining healthy and detangled hair.

Shampoo is used to clean the hair .

Dry hair? Look for a Moisturizing Shampoo.

For oily hair look for a Purifying Shampoo.

Conditioner is used to soften the hair , great for detangling and moisturizing.

The most important of all is water !

Adding water to your hair often is the #1 best way to healthy curls.

Sealing moisture in is best done with a leave in conditioner.

Moisturizing Shampoo and Conditioner

Pro tip: Try detangling with the conditioner in your hair before you rinse!

Water Spray Bottle

Leave in Conditioner

You have successfully gathered all the necessary tools, products. Now, it is time to cleanse your curls. Follow the steps below!

Whether in the shower or at the sink, saturate your hair thoroughly with water.

- Dispense two or three pumps of shampoo and apply it to your scalp, creating a lather.
- Proceed to scrub your scalp, avoiding excessive manipulation of the hair strands.
- If needed shampoo the hair twice or three times
- Rinse your hair, ensuring there are no suds left behind.

If your hair subs up a lot you know it is clean! If not go in for a second shampoo!

After you have finished shampooing, apply 2-5 pumps of conditioner to your hair.

With your hands split your hair into two or four sections. 2 sections for low to medium density 3 to 4 sections for medium to high density.

Add more condition to each section.

Focus on spreading the conditioner evenly from the roots to the tips of your hair in each section.

> Your hair should have a thick white coating of conditioner, as seen here!

Let the conditioner sit in your hair for 5-10 minutes to help soften and make detangling easier.
Using your fingers gently pull apart tangles in the hair.
If you can grab your detangling brush or comb and lightly detangle the hair.
Rinse conditioner throughly and get ready to section!

Here's what you need!

Nice Job!
   Once the conditioner has been rinsed. Prepare for sectioning, using your hair ties, a wide-tooth comb, and water.

Sectioning helps to separate the hair, making it easier to comb through. Instead of taking a large section, small sections help to detangle faster and cause less pain.

Using your spray bottle saturate your hair with water. Create a part using the wide-tooth comb, starting from your forehead and moving it towards the back.

To achieve a precise part, align the comb with your eyebrows and smoothly guide it from the front of your head to the back of your neck.

Following these steps, you have successfully divided your hair into two sections.

Secure one side into a ponytail using a hair tie.

Quick Tip
Use the tip of your comb to seperate the hair

Once the hair is parting down the middle, divide one section of the hair into two horizontal sections using the comb.

Start the comb at the top of the head down to right behind the ear. Secure these sections with two hair ties each.

Repeat the same parting process on the other side. You should now have four sections!

Sections should look similar to the photo here.

Great job sectioning! Now using your wide-tooth comb, bristle brush we will start to detangle.
Start with the one of the sections in the back.
Take the hair tie out and spray the hair down with water.
Then grab your leave in conditioner ,pump 2-5 pumps in your hand and work the product into the section of hair.
Using your fingers to gently pull the tangles apart.

Starting from the ends then moving upward as you go, brush the hair using your bristle brush.

Brushing the hair downward gently until the tangles are through.

You will know you are finished if you can take both your comb and brush and go smoothly through the section.

Repeat on the next few sections.

When you're done detangling you should be able to run your hair through without feeling any knots.

Continue these with the next 3 sections.

When finished you can add other styling products or create an amazing style!

When detangling the hair should look white with product!

Should i touch my hair?

    Make sure once the hair is set with the product, not to touch your hair! When your curls are wet, it's best to avoid touching them because this is when the hair is most vulnerable to frizz. Touching your curls or letting someone else touch your hair while it is wet and forming can break up the natural clumps, which are essential for defined, bouncy curls.

Allowing your curls to dry untouched helps lock in the curl pattern and maintain the integrity of your style. Once fully set and dry, you can fluff or adjust as needed without compromising the shape or finish.

Let's talk shrinkage!

Shrinkage is when curly or coily hair looks shorter than it really is because the curls tighten as the hair dries.

It's a natural characteristic of curly hair and shows how healthy and elastic the curls are.

Your curls may seem a little shorter ones your hair is dry but that is the beauty of curly hair, for your hair to have those amazing spirals you'll need to have some shrinkage!

CONGRATULATIONS

You've made it through your first detangle you did AMAZING!

Now let's keep up the good work, try practicing once a week or every 2 weeks to keep healthy curls spray your hair will water, separate your hair into sections and add leave in conditioner during the week to avoid excess tangling and to add moisture. The more we practice the easier it gets! See you next time!

Quiz Yourself

What have you been blessed with?

_____

Adding what is the #1 best way to healthy curls ?

_____

How long should conditioner sit in the hair ?

_____

How many sections should you have before you start detangling?

_____

Quiz Yourself

What words can help define what type of hair you have ?

_____

What is essential to your hair routine?

_____

What are the names of the guides throughout the book?

_____

What does sectioning do ?

_____

Cross Word Puzzle

```
T B S H A M P O O F H D
C T R O P W A T E R Z E
O Q R P O R O S I T Y N
I B C U R L S B H I Y S
L T E X T U R E O E P I
S X F P A T T E R N O T
C O N D I T I O N E R Y
M O L D E T A N G L E B
```

Find the following words in the puzzle.

CONDITIONER	POROSITY	CURLS
DENSITY	WATER	DETANGLE
PATTERN	SHAMPOO	
COILS	TEXTURE	

Find the missing wide tooth comb!

Somewhere along the pages you will find this wide tooth comb in an unexpected places! Once found circle all the hiding combs! There are 5 missing combs!

Answer Page

1. Gorgeous curls and coils
2. Adding water to your hair
3. 5-10 minutes
4. 4 sections
5. Texture, density, and porosity
6. Matthew, Lisa, and Monique
7. Helps separate the hair get it ready to detangle

```
T B S H A M P O O F H D
O T R O P W A T E R Z E
O Q R P O R O S I T Y N
I B C U R L S B H I Y S
L T E X T U R E O E P I
S X F P A T T E R N O T
C O N D I T I O N E R Y
M O L D E T A N G L E B
```